THE

Conservative's

DICTIONARY

THE
Conservative's
DICTIONARY

TODD DOMKE AND GERRY LANGE

Illustrations by Marty Riskin

St. Martin's Griffin

New York

Library of Congress Cataloging-in-Publication Data

Domke, Todd.

The conservative's dictionary / by Tom [i.e. Todd] Domke & Gerry Lange.

p.   cm.

ISBN 0-312-14101-7

1. Conservatism—United States—Humor.   2. United States—Politics and government—1993–   —Humor. 3. United States—Politics and government—1993–   —Caricatures and cartoons.   4. Political satire, American.   5. American wit and humor, Pictorial.   I. Lange, Gerry.   II. Title.

E839.5.D66   1996

973'.0207—dc20   95-44833

                                                             CIP

Design by Bonni Leon-Berman

First St. Martin's Griffin Edition: April 1996

10 9 8 7 6 5 4 3 2 1

For my parents.
—T. L. D.

For C. and C.
—G. W. L.

Introduction

Liberals used to laugh at conservatives as uptight fuddy-duddies with pin-striped suits and cheap haircuts—country clubbers with no sense of humor. If this describes you, well, thanks for buying this book...and please buy some for your less affluent friends.

The truth, however, is that most conservatives live and work in the real world, and they have a well-developed sense of humor for a good reason: How else can you survive in the wacky world liberalism has created?

And liberals are such *easy* targets.

With Rush Limbaugh and Newt Gingrich directing the play, and Bill Clinton and Ted Kennedy writing the script, conservatives find something to chuckle at every time they look around.

First, you have Rush. It's just plain fun to watch him having fun poking fun at liberals. Even more fun is watching liberals watch Rush. Invite a few to your house sometime (if you can catch them when they're not busy awarding Pulitzer prizes to each other), turn on Rush's TV program, and observe. They don't know how to react. They can't simply dismiss him; he has too large an audience, including well-educated, intelligent viewers who take him seriously. They can't ignore him; he's *everywhere*. They can't laugh at themselves because they take themselves very, very seriously. So, they're usually reduced to making lame jokes about him being oversize. Of course he's oversize; day after day, program after program, he's been eating their lunch.

Then there's Newt. He's aggressive, smart, articulate, shrewd, gutsy, and powerful—all the things liberals wish they were. But it's no longer their day; it's probably not even their century. They're trapped in a Brave Newt World of limited government and fewer bureaucrats. If this continues, how will they ever succeed in imposing the metric system on the rest of us?

Sure, they still have Bill Clinton and his Arkansas travelers, but is that all there is, my friend? He's leading them into the political wilderness, where for the next forty years they may have to survive on Brie from heaven. Clinton has managed to assemble the most horrifying cabinet since Doctor Caligari, and then, in case these characters weren't funny enough, made Joycelyn Elders the Surgeon General. As for Clinton's closest personal advisors, in case you want to know what they look like, just check the Wanted posters at your local post office.

Ted Kennedy is the frosting on the cake. Sometime in the past, his inner child escaped out into the great playpen of life. Where would conservative humor be without his prodigious appetites, sexual escapades, and overall self-indulgence? He's the perfect icon for modern liberalism: oversexed, overrated, and over-the-hill.

One final thought: Never forget that humor is the assault weapon liberals fear most.

So...read...enjoy...and spread the word.

A

ACLU:

American Civil Liberties Union. A bunch of liberal lawyers trying to wrong rights, invent rights, and on rare occasions even do what's right.

ADULTERY:

What Bill Clinton always thought was plural for adult.

ADVOCATE:

According to the media, a liberal proponent of a liberal policy; a conservative proponent of a conservative policy is called a lobbyist.

AGRICULTURE SUBSIDY:

Ted Kennedy's proposal for the malt, hops, olive, and ice industries.

ALIENATION:

Nation that liberals feel most patriotic about.

ANDROGYNOUS:

Being both male and female. The ultimate goal of radical feminists, because it would enable a woman to marry herself.

ANIMAL RIGHTS MOVEMENT:

Activists who believe that the only creature that should ever be put on a leash is a fellow consenting adult—but not one wearing fur.

APPEASEMENT:

"Belief that if you keep on throwing steaks to a tiger, the tiger will turn into a vegetarian."

—*Heywood Broun*

APRÈS MOI, LE DÉLUGE:

"Following me, the deluge," famous words of Louis XV. Compare to Hillary Clinton's comment "*Après nous, les deludes*," or "The deluded follow us."

ARROGANCE:

Liberal self-esteem.

ASSAD, HAFEZ:
Leader of Syria. A vicious dictator who, given the classic choice between two evils, will choose both.

ASSAULT WEAPON:
(1) Liberal term for any gun that doesn't fire water.
(2) What liberals call Newt Gingrich's mouth.

ASSISTED SUICIDE:
(1) An alternative death-style. (2) The wave good-bye of the future.

ATHEISM:
Spiritual anorexia; devout belief in disbelief.

AVANT-GARDE:
Fiercely independent, individualistic artists and intellectuals who lead the charge for government grants.

AVERAGE AMERICAN:
The most praised and influential person who never lived.

B

BABBLE:

A confusion of tongues, from the biblical story about the Tower of Babel—a classic example of bilingual education at work.

BAKKER, ROBERT:

Famous paleontologist who has advanced the theory that dinosaurs were warm-blooded animals. He is known for his clarity of thinking, evidenced by his answer when asked his next goal: "I want to discover a voracious, small-minded predator and name it after the IRS."

BALDWIN, ALEC:

Actor and political activist who campaigns for liberal Democrats. Mr. Baldwin is married to Kim Basinger,

TAXEROPTERUS

which raises the question, "Why do good things happen to bad people?"

BANANA PEEL:
Official fruit of the Clinton administration.

BASIC RESEARCH:
"What I am doing when I don't know what I am doing."
—Wernher von Braun

BAYWATCH:
A TV show conservatives like to recommend to feminist friends.

BELTWAY:
Highway around Washington, D.C., separating the federal government from reality.

BENTSEN, LLOYD:
Former secretary of the treasury under President Clinton. At White House news conferences, the two were addressed as Bentsen & Hedges.

BIBLE:
Basic text of both Judaism and Christianity, forbidden in public schools on the grounds that it might cause morality.

BIDEN, JOSEPH:

Delaware senator whose candidacy for the Democratic presidential nomination collapsed when the media exposed instances of plagiarism. It was all just a simple, human error—he misinterpreted the Copyright Law as a Right to Copy Law.

BILINGUALISM:

A system in which languages other than English are encouraged and accepted in government and culture. Liberals strongly support bilingualism because anything they say sounds more sensible in a foreign language.

BIPARTISAN:

When both political parties feel it's necessary to be pleasant because they have to endorse something unpleasant but necessary.

BISEXUAL:

Two for the spice of one. Or, two for the vice of one. Depending on your point of view.

BITE THE BALLOT:

"What doctors told congressmen who supported the Clinton health-care plan."

—*David Keene*

BLATHER:

A style of rhetoric perfected by liberal "serious thinkers" who can speak nonsense without fear of media ridicule. *Example*: "Life is an endless unfolding, and if we wish it to be, an endless process of self-discovery, an endless and unpredictable dialogue between our own potentialities and the life situations in which we find ourselves."

—John Gardner, founder of Common Cause, speaking at Stanford University

BLUE SMOKE & MIRRORS:

(1) Book by Jack Germond and Jules Witcover about the 1980 presidential campaign. It refers to the way campaigns use "image" to reflect, obscure, and magnify reality. (2) It also refers to Ted Kennedy's bedroom, which has blue-smoke incense and a mirror above the bed warning, OBJECTS MAY APPEAR LARGER THAN THEY ARE.

BOBBITT, LORENA:

A woman on the cutting edge of feminism.

BORN WITH A SILVER HAIRBALL IN HER MOUTH:

Excuse to explain the poor taste so often exhibited by former Texas Governor Ann Richards.

BOSNIA:
Some sort of country where several sides have been fighting some kind of war over something.

BOXER REBELLION:
Incident when Clinton's beleaguered PR staff threatened to resign if he didn't keep his underwear to himself.

BOY SCOUTS OF AMERICA:
As liberals see it, a homophobic, paternalistic, chauvinistic, paramilitary organization of brainwashed young boys who take loyalty oaths, carry assault knives, defile wilderness by camping in it, and reveal their basic sexist belief that women are the weaker sex when they aggressively help an elderly woman across a street.

BRADLEY, BILL:
Monotoned Democratic senator and former basketball star who decided not to run for reelection because he was going to lose anyway. Thought by the media to be one of very few liberals actually *electable* as president because he sounds too dull to be dangerous.

BRAUN, CAROL MOSELEY:
U.S. senator (D-IL) who every time she opens her mouth makes people think fondly of mimes.

BREAD AND CIRCUSES:
Something offered to pacify the masses. In ancient Rome, to suppress discontent among the common people, emperors ordered the distribution of bread and staged elaborate entertainments in the Colosseum— where violence, gore, and death provided a distraction from the burdens of everyday life. Today, we have *The Ricki Lake Show.*

BREAKFAST OF CHAMPIONS:
To Rush Limbaugh, having a liberal over-easy.

BREAST STROKE:
(1) What Ted Kennedy claimed he did to save himself at Chappaquiddick. (2) What Bob Packwood claimed he did not remember doing.

BROWN, JERRY:
Former Democratic governor of California, who once said: "I see the world in very fluid, contradictory,

emerging, interconnected terms, and with that kind of circuitry I just don't feel the need to say what is going to happen or will not happen." *Note*: This is an actual quote. Really.

BROWN, MURPHY:

TV's idea of a role model for unwed mothers—if they own an $800,000 Washington, D.C., townhouse, can afford a full-time live-in nanny, and have an income of $300,000 a year.

BROWN, RON:

Secretary of commerce under Clinton who claims that he is innocent of wrongdoing because he hasn't been convicted yet.

B.S.:

See Streisand, Barbra.

BUREAUCRATS:

"The only people in the world who say nothing, and mean it."

—*James Boren*

C

CABINET THAT LOOKS LIKE AMERICA:
Candidate Bill Clinton's promise to appoint as diverse
a group of millionaire lawyers as possible.

CAMBRIDGE, MASSACHUSETTS:
The Alamo of democratic socialism.

CAMPBELL, BEN NIGHTHORSE:
(1) Colorado senator who switched to the Republican
Party, explaining that his name was Nighthorse, not
Crazyhorse. (2) The first Campbell to jump *out* of the
soup.

CAMP DAVID:
The first refuge of a scoundrel.

CAN OF WORMS:
A restroom filled with TV executives.

CAPITAL GAINS TAX:
A tax on selling something for profit, based on the liberal economic theory that if you don't punish success,
it might spread.

CAPITAL PUNISHMENT:

"You've *got* to execute people—how else are they going to learn?"

—*Mort Sahl*

CAPITOL ROTUNDA:

(1) Large central area beneath the Capitol Dome.
(2) Jack Germond.

CARDINAL RULE OF THE MEDIA:

"If you give me six lines written by the most honest man, I will find something in them to hang him."

—*Cardinal Richelieu*

CAREER POLITICIAN:

Incumbent who stays in office until he's recumbent.

CARPE DIEM:

Latin for "seize the day." Mistranslated by Clinton's press staff, none of whom has a classical education, as "carp every day."

CARTER, JIMMY:

Thirty-ninth president of the United States and the finest poet ever to come out of Plains, Georgia. As a

volunteer for Habitat for Humanity, he now pounds
nails into houses instead of hammering the U.S.
economy.

CARTER, LILLIAN:
Jimmy Carter's mother, best known for saying,
"Sometimes when I look at my children, I say to
myself, 'Lillian, you should have stayed a virgin.'"

CARVILLE, JAMES:
Strategist for Bill Clinton and chief political advisor to
many Democratic losers; the Wile E. Coyote of
Democratic politics.

CASTRO, FIDEL:
Communist dictator who Fideled while Cuba's
economy burned.

CBS NEWS:
Where viewers turn not to be informed but to be infected.

CELEBRITY:
"Someone whose name is worth more than his services."

—*Daniel Boorstin*

CHANGE:
Clinton's 1992 campaign mantra. Voters didn't realize he was talking about his own convictions. "Most of us learned some time ago that if you don't like [President Clinton's] position on a particular issue, you simply need to wait a few weeks."

—*Congressman David Obey (D-WI)*

CHAOS THEORY:
Clinton management style.

CHAPPAQUIDDICK:
Where Mary Jo Kopechne and Camelot died.

CHECKERS:
(1) Richard Nixon's dog. (2) A game Clinton cronies teach other inmates.

CHECKS AND BALANCES:
A reference to the House banking scandal, where there were far too many checks and far too few balances.

CHINA:
Model country for labor unions and liberalism, because all of its jobs pay the minimum wage.

CHRISTOPHER, WARREN:
American secretary of state who seems to have died sometime during the Carter administration but who continues to function because nobody told him. In Latin, Warren Christopher's name is pronounced "Rigor Mortis."

CIA:
Central Intelligence Agency, the only federal agency ever established with intelligence as its goal.

CIVIL RIGHTS:
Term that once described equal opportunity, dignity, and respect. It now covers that high school chucklehead who demands the right to wear an eyebrow ring.

CLARIFY:
"A term used by presidential candidates when they want to obfuscate."

—Michael Barone

CLASS WARFARE:
How wealthy Democratic strategists try to pit the poor against their own self-interests.

CLIFF DWELLERS:
Prehistoric natives who built their dwellings high up in canyon walls. Identified as "Early Liberals" because they lived with their heads in the clouds.

CLIFT, ELEANOR:
Newsweek's unofficial spokeswoman for the Clinton administration. To be kind, conservatives call her a

liar; otherwise, they would have to assume she's so stupid she actually believes what she says.

CLINTON, WILLIAM JEFFERSON (BILL):
(1) Proof that anyone can grow up, or not grow up, and become president of the United States. (2) The Doctor Kevorkian of the Democratic Party.

COBAIN, KURT:
Troubled rock star who committed suicide. Called "the voice of his generation," although he was usually incomprehensible because of drugs or alcohol.

COCAINE:
"God's way of saying you're making too much money."
—*Robin Williams*

COINCIDENCE:
Concurrence of circumstances often appropriate to one another. *Examples:*
a) Forty-three cents of every dollar earned by the average taxpayer goes to government. Bill Clinton was elected with 43 percent of the vote!
b) The name "Bill Clinton" has eleven letters in it. The word *chucklehead* also has eleven letters!
c) The odds of Hillary Clinton turning her $1,000 in cattle futures into $100,000 without insider trading

information was calculated to be four in one billion. The odds of Hillary's health-care boondoggle being enacted into law while Republicans control Congress are also four in one billion!

COLLECTIVISM:
"Not a system in which people are considered equal, but a system where all people are considered alike."

—*P. J. O'Rourke*

COLLEGE:
What used to be called high school.

COLUMBUS, CHRISTOPHER:
(1) Italian explorer who discovered America in 1492. Five hundred years later, liberals have yet to discover it.

(2) To liberals, Columbus is the angry white male who began genocide against Native Americans. To high school students, he's some guy who started a parade in New York City.

COMIC RELIEF:
Annual telethon produced by mostly liberal comedians to show that they care, deeply care, very deeply care, care a whole lot, about their images as caring celebrities.

COMMON CAUSE:
Lobbyists lobbying against lobbyists lobbying.

COMMON SENSE:
Know-how that fewer and fewer know now.

COMMUNISM:
(1) Another contemptible -ism on its way to being a wasm. (2) "We are not without accomplishment. We have managed to distribute poverty equally."
  —*Nguyen Co Thach, Vietnamese Foreign Minister*

COMMUNIST CHIC:
"Wherever Communists rule, the results are poverty, misery, refugees and death. But let a tyrant call himself 'Marxist' and suddenly he's a soulful

revolutionary and cult hero. In America, journalists and academics and Pete Seeger will line up to sing his praises and denounce his foes. Communist chic can make even the most homicidal thug seem appealing and full of charm. Ted Kennedy gushed that Leonid Brezhnev—a leading practitioner of state terror, the tyrant who sent the tanks into Prague and Sakharov into exile—was 'a warm individual, highly intelligent, highly aware, with a sense of humor, completely at ease, very informal...completely committed to peace.' Add a beard and a red suit, and you've got Santa Claus."

—Jeff Jacoby

COMMUNIST MANIFESTO:

A declaration of Communist principles written and distributed by Karl Marx and Friedrich Engels, who stated, "The theory of Communism can be summed up in one sentence: abolish all private property." They still kept the royalties.

COMPASSION:

Liberal rationale for compulsory charity. "A politician who commends himself as 'caring' and 'sensitive' because he wants to expand the government's charitable programs is merely saying that he's willing to try to do good with other people's money. Who isn't?"

—P. J. O'Rourke

COMPUTER:
A machine with above-average intelligence, proven by the fact that no one has ever caught a computer watching *Beverly Hills 90210*.

COMPUTER DATING:
Nerds desperately seeking new software.

CONDESCENDING:
Stretching exercise for liberals.

CONGRESSIONAL BUDGET OFFICE:
"Nonpartisan" group of "experts" who analyze the proposed federal budget and try to predict its effects on the deficit and the economy using complex econometric models, powerful computers, and an ample supply of goat entrails.

CONSENSUS:
A working majority that agrees to do the wrong thing for the best intentions.

CONSTITUENTS:
The individual components of something larger. For example, special interest groups are the separate parts of the Democratic Party; when assembled, they make the Democratic ass whole.

CONSUMER CONFIDENCE:
A leading indicator of economic activity that coincidentally plummets every April 15.

CONSUMER FRAUD:
Ralph Nader.

COOLIDGE, CALVIN:
"The first President to discover that what the American people want is to be left alone."

—Will Rogers

COP:
According to one source, an acronym derived from the English "Constable On Patrol." The liberal acronym for police officers is a little different: "Dangerous Armed Mercenaries Needing Civilian Oversight Permanently," or DAMNCOP.

CORE VALUES:
For Bill Clinton, his latest poll results.

COUNCIL OF ECONOMIC ADVISORS:

A panel of experts serving under the president with the aim of managing the economy. Under Clinton, they stage-manage it.

COUNTERCULTURE McGOVERNIKS:

Term coined by Newt Gingrich to describe Bill and Hillary Clinton. Liberals were incensed that Gingrich gave a Soviet twist to the accepted American slur, McGovern*ite*.

COUNTRY-WESTERN CAMPAIGN MUSIC:

Down-home songs selected by a candidate to let voters know who he really is and what he feels down deep. Possibilities for Clinton's reelection campaign include: "Why Do You Believe Me When I Tell You That I Love You, When You Know I've Been a Liar All My Life?"; "I'll Marry You Tomorrow, But Let's Honeymoon Tonight"; "Get Your Tongue Outta My Mouth 'Cause I'm Kissing You Good-bye"; "If Fingerprints Showed Up on Skin, Wonder Whose I'd Find on You?"; and the final contender, "It Ain't Love, But It Ain't Bad."

COURTESY:

A word meaning "politeness," a kind of behavior rumored to still survive in modern-day America in a few isolated pockets of the South and Midwest. The last known case of it in New York City was reported in 1953.

COUSTEAU, JACQUES:
Marine biologist who cautions, "The environmental movement is being poisoned by becoming part of politics." (It isn't doing much good for politics, either.)

CRIME:
A violation of the law. To liberals, if you're poor, law-breaking is caused by poverty; if you're a Republican, it's caused by wealth.

CRISIS:
What liberals call a problem when they want more money.

CRISTOPHE:
Celebrity hair stylist who coiffed President Clinton on Air Force One while the plane sat on a runway at Los Angeles airport. When the haircut sparked controversy, Cristophe defended the president: "Do you really think that Hillary or Bill Clinton, from what you can see, is very concerned about their appearance?"

CRITICS:

Derived from *cri,* French for whine, and *tics* for blood-sucking parasites. Literally: whining, bloodsucking parasites.

CUBA:

(1) Latin American island nation located off the southern coast of the United States. Its main export is refugees. (2) Communist country for which radical American college students will do anything, except live there.

CULT:

"Any religion without political power."

—*Tom Wolfe*

CULTURE:

"Roughly, anything we do and the monkeys don't."

—*Lord Raglan*

Contrast with *counterculture:* What monkeys *could* do, but don't.

CYNICISM:

What liberals call realism.

D

DANGEROUS LIAISONS:
(1) President John Kennedy's affair with Judith Exner, girlfriend of mobster Sam Giancana. (2) Robert Kennedy's affair with Marilyn Monroe. (3) Almost any date with Ted Kennedy.

DANSON, TED:
Proof that liberalism causes bad movies.

DASCHLE, TOM:
Senate minority leader (D-SD) who ran for office favoring the Balanced Budget Amendment and emphasizing his support for it, then changed his mind when his vote would have made a difference. He apparently suffers from multiple personalities, at least one of them dishonest.

DECADENCE:
A state of decay or decline, e.g., California.

DECISIVENESS, CLINTON-STYLE:
"President Clinton is reported to be contemplating a notion to develop an initiative to consider the possibil-

ity of formulating an intention to assemble a frame-
work, which could, under certain circumstances, be
used to develop the foundation for a possible plan to
devise a tentative policy ..."

—*National Review*

DEFICIT SPENDING:
The gap between what voters pay in taxes and what
politicians boast about bringing home to the voters.

DELLUMS, RON:
Looney Democratic congressman from Berkeley,
California, who excused the Russian invasion of
Afghanistan by saying: "Look at it from the Russians'
point of view—they only want a stable neighbor." A
desire they share with Dellums's own neighbors. (The
Democratic leadership has assigned him to the Intelligence Committee in the hope some might rub off on
him.)

DEMOCRACY:
A form of government in which people are free to
elect their representatives, who in turn are free to
ignore the wishes of the people who elected them, in
which case the people are free to chuck them out and
elect new representatives who will also ignore their
wishes.

DEMOCRATIC NATIONAL COMMITTEE:

The Jamaican bobsled team of politics.

DEMOCRATIC PARTY:

Once-proud party of FDR; now the reactionary party of FEAR. "If Thomas Edison had invented the electric light in the age of the welfare state, the Democrats would immediately introduce a bill to protect the candlemaking industry. The Democrat ticket would propose a tax on electricity. Ralph Nader would warn that electricity can kill. And at least one news report would begin, 'The candlemaking industry was threatened today.'"

—Newt Gingrich

DEPARTMENT OF THE INTERIOR:

"Where else but in Washington would they call the department in charge of everything outdoors the Department of the Interior?"

—Ronald Reagan

DEPENDENCE ON GOVERNMENT:

"The opiate of the masses."

—Richard Armey, House Majority Leader

DERIVATIVES:

William Kennedy Smith, Patrick Kennedy, Joseph Kennedy...

DETERRENCE:

Discouraging an enemy from attacking. As Oliver Cromwell said, "A man-of-war is the best ambassador." Unless Jeanne Kirkpatrick is available.

DICKY FLATT TEST:

(1) Senator Phil Gramm's criterion for deciding whether a federal program is worthwhile, i.e., whether a working friend of Gramm's named Dicky Flatt would want his hard-earned taxes to pay for it. (2) A challenge to Ted Kennedy to try abstaining for a whole weekend.

DICTATORSHIP:
Government that begins with "I, the people."

DISABILITY ACT:
When Ted Kennedy wore a neck brace immediately after Chappaquiddick.

DISCIPLINE:
What they can't even *spell* in many public schools.

DISCRIMINATION:
In the words of Yasmine Bleeth, star of *Baywatch,* "Tall, skinny women can get breast implants, and they become perfect. But women who are small and curvy can't get leg extensions. That isn't fair!" Apparently, 5'5" actresses can't get IQ extensions either.

DISPOSABLE INCOME:
How liberal congressmen refer to the U.S. economy.

DISTORTION:
A charge hurled by an incumbent against his challenger whenever the challenger quotes the incumbent.

DIVERSITY:
"When liberals of all ethnic persuasions get together."
—*Rush Limbaugh*

DIVERSITY QUOTA:
The idea that the Midwest would be a whole lot more civilized if it were more like New York City.

DOCUMENTARY:
What they call the movie *Deliverance* in Arkansas.

DODDERING FOOL:
Christopher Dodd, (D-CT).

DON'T ASK, DON'T TELL:
A clause Ted Kennedy slips into his prenuptial agreements.

DORNAN, BOB:
Conservative congressman (R-CA). Liberals think he's nicknamed "B-1 Bob" for championing the B-1 bomber. Actually, it's because he has one parked in his garage.

DRAMA:
According to Alfred Hitchcock, life with the dull bits cut out. Unless it's PBS, in which case it's life with the exciting parts cut out.

DRESS CODE:

In modern high schools, the requirement that girls wear shirts, boys wear shoes, and teachers wear bullet-proof vests.

DRUNK DRIVING LAWS:

Laws forbidding anyone from driving while drunk, theoretically opposed by liberals because drunk drivers don't kill people—cars do.

DUCT TAPE:

What Barbra Streisand should use instead of lipstick.

DUKAKIS, MICHAEL:

(1) Democratic presidential nominee who was told by Ted Koppel, "Governor, you just don't get it." So, in November 1988 the voters gave it to him. (2) The kind of guy you'd want in your foxhole—if you wanted to study soil erosion.

DUTY, HONOR, COUNTRY:
Three words that evoke patriotism. If a liberal
Democrat uses one of these words in a speech, he's in
a serious fight for reelection. If he uses two, his
polling results are bleak. If he uses all three, he's
preparing to switch parties.

E

ECOLOGY:
Liberal theology.

ECONOMIC GROWTH:
Something liberals believe is caused by government
action, the way wet pavement causes rain.

ECONOMISTS:
"People who see something work in practice and wonder if it would work in theory."

—*Ronald Reagan*

EDUCATIONAL REFORM:
Homework would be a start.

EGALITARIANISM:
"Envy masquerading as philosophy."

—*George F. Will*

EHRLICH, PAUL:
Population doomsayer who predicted that by now the world would be experiencing rising death rates (they've actually fallen), widespread oil shortages, mass starvation everywhere, killer smogs in Los Angeles, and rising ocean levels that would swamp coastal cities...once again proving that it's easy to predict the future; it's just difficult to be right.

EINSTEIN, ALBERT:
Physicist who discovered both the general and special laws of relativity, two of the fundamental truths about the workings of the universe. His third

great discovery, unfortunately overlooked in the excitement surrounding publication of general and special relativity, was: "Whatever you do, don't vote for Bill Clinton."

ELDERS, JOYCELYN:
Controversial surgeon general fired by President Clinton for suggesting that students take sex education into their own hands.

ELECTIVE OFFICE:
Like elective surgery, but instead of wearing stitches in public, you leave the public in stitches.

ELECTRIC CHAIR:
The only piece of furniture that comes with a lifetime guarantee.

ELOQUENCE:
Telling people what they want to hear before they know what they want to hear.

EMBEZZLE:
To appropriate someone's funds without their consent. *Synonym: withholding taxes.*

ENDANGERED SPECIES:
Any animal that provides a rare taste experience when served skinned with lots of salt.

ENTITLEMENT:
In England, a system that awards ranks of nobility to favored persons, giving special powers and privileges over common people. In America, a system that gives on favored persons special powers and privileges over taxpayers.

ENTREPRENEUR:
"From the French *entreprendre*, 'to undertake.' One who undertakes new ventures in the private sector. In a very different sense, liberal politicians and bureaucrats are also undertakers. They bury entrepreneurs in taxes and red tape."

—*Louis H. T. Dehmlow*

ENVIRONMENTALIST:
(1) Activist who believes only beavers have the right to fell trees and construct dams. (2) Someone with a profound and abiding respect for all living things, except humans.

ENVY:
Liberalism's basic philosophical principle arising from the fear that someone, somewhere, might be more successful. Worse yet, they might deserve to be.

EQUALITY:
Sameness in status, something liberals want—for others. "We who are liberal and progressive know that the poor are our equals in every sense except that of being equal to us."

—*Lionel Trilling*

ESTATE TAX:
The death penalty for people guilty of success.

EVIL EMPIRE:
Time/Warner.

EVOLUTION:
Nature gone ape.

EXCOMMUNICATE:
What radical feminists want to do to the pope.

EXISTENTIALISM:
A philosophy that says that before anyone can find meaning in life, he must first experience the "nausea" caused by the realization that life is absurd—a stage reached by most Americans after only two years of the Clinton administration.

EXPERT:

(1) A knowledgeable person who "should be on tap but never on top."

—Winston Churchill

(2) "One who has made all the mistakes which can be made in a very narrow field."

—Niels Bohr

EXTINCTION:

What ecologists not only predict but hope for, so they can say with finality, "I told you so."

EXTREMIST:

Democratic catchword to tar any and all conservative ideas or candidates. According to the liberal media, liberals are never extremist or "ultra-liberal"; they are "committed." And they should be.

F

FACE-OFF:

Request made by numerous callers to C-SPAN whenever Patricia Schroeder testifies at a congressional hearing.

FACTS:
Sorry, this word is not in any political dictionary.

FAILURE OF LIBERALISM:
"You can't teach an old dogma new tricks."

—*Dorothy Parker*

FAIRNESS:
Liberal euphemism for "stick 'em up!"

FALUDI, SUSAN:
Enraged feminist and author of *Backlash,* which offers advice on how to attract, catch, and keep a man, plus twenty-three recipes for how to prepare and cook him once you have him.

FANATIC:
"A man that does what he thinks the Lord would do if He knew the facts of the case."

—*Finley Peter Dunne*

FARM PROGRAMS:

Federal government subsidies that pay farmers not to produce. If only the National Endowment for the Arts and the National Endowment for the Humanities worked the same way.

FARRAKHAN, LOUIS:

Head of the Black Muslims who no longer practices anti-Semitism because he no longer needs the practice.

FATHER:

A man who wishes he was as sure of anything as his children are of everything.

FATHER'S DAY:

An occasion where picking out a card is much harder, now that there are so many categories: Father's Day cards, Stepfather's Day, Absentee Father's Day, Deadbeat Father's Day, Second Family Father's Day, First Fathers Once-Removed Day, Fathers Who Dress Like Mothers Day...

—adapted from "Mallard Fillmore" by Bruce Tinsley

FEAR:

The emotion Democrats appeal to when they fear losing an election.

FEDERAL BUREAUCRAT:
Someone who does nothing badly.

FIRST AMENDMENT:
"It says that members of religious groups, no matter how small or unpopular, shall have the right to hassle you in airports."

—Dave Barry

FLOWERS, GENNIFER:
The state deflower of Arkansas.

FOB:
Acronym for "Friend Of Bill," an early supporter of Bill Clinton for President. After two years in office and countless investigations, the acronym now also refers to "Freeloaders On Bail" and "Full Of Bull."

FOGGY BOTTOM:
Nickname for the U.S. State Department headquarters in Washington, D.C. As possible synonyms for *foggy* and *bottom*, the thesaurus suggests *bewildered, ass.*

FONDA, JANE:
Actress, radical feminist, radical antinuclear activist, radical environmentalist, radical proponent of popula-

tion control, radical supporter of the Viet Cong, radical champion of multiculturalism, radical enemy of the U.S. military, radical defender of the rights of criminals, radical promoter, sponsor, and spokesperson of radicalism. A few years ago Ms. Fonda caught herself a rich husband and is now Ted Turner's main squeeze.

FOOL:
According to an Arabian proverb, a fool is known by six things: anger without cause; speech without profit; change without progress; inquiry without object; putting trust in a stranger; and mistaking foes for friends. Actually, there's a seventh, but it applies only to Yasir Arafat: stubble without beard.

FORCED BUSSING:
A policy once strongly supported by Bob Packwood.

FORD, CARTER, AND NIXON:
According to Bob Dole, "See No Evil, Hear No Evil, and Evil."

FOREIGN AID:
Money taken from middle-class people in the United States and given to the powerful elites of other countries to make it even easier for them to send their children to expensive American universities.

FOUL BALL:
The Clinton Inaugural bash.

FOUNDER:
Politically correct term for "founding fathers."
Founder is far more suitable for liberals because it also means "sink to the depths," which they often do.

FOURTH ESTATE:
News media. The term is derived from the old notion of social "estates," or ranks. The first three estates were the Estate Noble, the Estate Clerical, and the Estate Common. Because of its power, the media became known as the fourth estate, or the Estate Peeping Tom.

FRANCE:
A nation that views sex humorously and Jerry Lewis seriously. (What do you expect? They eat snails.)

FREE LUNCH:
There's no such thing—unless you're in school, or on welfare, or in prison, or work in an embassy, or break into a grocery store during a riot, or...

FREUDIAN SLIP:
An accidental misspeaking that reveals a subconscious thought. Barney Frank accused Dick Armey of it when the Majority Leader said "Barney Fag." Other examples: President Rodham, Jesse Jinxon, Cunning Chung, Oliver Stoned, Senator Dianne Frankenstein, and Al Notsosharpton.

FUTURE SHOCK:
(1) Term coined by Newt Gingrich's futurist friends, the Tofflers, to describe the dizzying rate of change transforming society. (2) "What strikes Democratic strategists when they realize that population growth in the south and west will make the electoral college even more conservative after redistricting in the year 2000."

—Joseph Gaylord

G

GAFFE:
When politicians accidentally say what people are thinking.

GALBRAITH, JOHN KENNETH:
Liberalism's favorite economist of the 1960s and '70s because he provided an intellectual justification for

overregulating the free market: Consumers aren't really free to choose because their desires are manipulated and controlled by advertising. But he was never able to explain why in China, which allowed no advertising of any kind, everybody smoked.

GAVEL:
Device used by judges to pound some sense into the heads of lawyers.

GAY:
Lively and merry. (Remember, this is a *conservative's* dictionary.)

GAYS IN THE MILITARY:
Bill Clinton's surprise plan to improve the decor in those dreadfully tacky military barracks.

GENERATION X:
McKids.

GEPHARDT, RICHARD:
House minority leader whose personality is proof that nature doesn't *always* fill a vacuum.

GERGEN, DAVID:
Consummate White House insider, Republican disloyalist, and Washington's human weather vane—

a reliable indicator of which way the wind blew yesterday.

GERMANY:
A theme park for authoritarians.

GHALI, BOUTROS-BOUTROS:
Secretary-Secretary General of the United-United Nations; proud father of Boutros-Boutros-Boutros Ghali.

GIULIANI, RUDOLPH:
"Republican" mayor of New York who endorsed Democrat Mario Cuomo for reelection over Republican candidate and eventual winner George Pataki. After the election, Giuliani explained that he was just kidding.

GLOBAL WARMING/COOLING:
The proposition that the average temperature of the earth is rising, or maybe dropping, or maybe staying the same, or maybe going sideways, so everyone should

give up cars and electricity and accept masochism as an alternative lifestyle. This from people who can't tell us for sure whether it's going to rain tomorrow.

GOLF:
(1) "A game in which you yell fore, shoot six, and write down five."
—Paul Harvey
(2) A game Ted Kennedy is *not* referring to when he whispers, "Would you like to play a round?"

GOOD INTENTIONS:
The liberal's all-purpose apology for utter disaster. "No one would remember the Good Samaritan if he'd only had good intentions—he had money, too."
—Margaret Thatcher

GORBACHEV, MIKHAIL:
Last dictator of the Soviet empire, admired by swooning liberals to the bitter end. He tried to save Communism by introducing capitalistic incentives— which is like trying to save your marriage by introducing your mistress to your wife.

GORE, AL:
First android vice president. "Al" is an abbreviation for Alien Life form.

"GOTCHA" JOURNALISM:

Term used by people naive enough to think there's some other kind of journalism.

GREAT SOCIETY:

(1) Wasteful, bureaucratic set of social programs pushed through Congress by Lyndon Johnson.
(2) Proof that the evil that men do lives after them.

GREENPEACE:

Fanatical ecologists whose unofficial credo is *Save the planet—kill yourself.*

GREENSPAN, ALAN:

Chairman of the Federal Reserve, known for speaking in vague economic platitudes. He's already written his own epitaph: "I am guardedly optimistic about the next world, but cognizant of the downside risk."

—*Wall Street Journal*

GRIDLOCK:

When partisan conflict between Congress and the White House prevents anything from getting done. When it stops Democratic tax hikes, boondoggles, and bureaucracy, it's known as *gladlock*.

GROSS DOMESTIC PRODUCT:

Howard Stern.

GROWN IN OFFICE:

Phrase used by liberal columnists to praise conservatives who sell out their principles once they're elected. Compare to *groan in office*, which refers to the sound coming from the Oval Office whenever Bill Clinton receives new polling numbers or a female visitor.

GUILT:

Liberal joy.

GULLIBLE'S TRAVELS:
Warren Christopher's itinerary.

GUMP, FORREST:
Movie character famous for his simple but profound epigrams, e.g., "Life is like a box of chocolates. You never know what you're gonna get," and "Stupid is as Roseanne does."

GUN CONTROL:
Laws that aim to control wicked guns that fire themselves at innocent people. Liberals advocate that guns caught doing so should be beaten savagely into plowshares. Since plowshares are extremely sharp, however, the next step is plowshare control laws.

H

HALF-TRUTH:
In a Michael Kinsley diatribe, a very generous portion.

HALLUCINATION:
A liberal politician's "vision" for America.

HANDS-ON EXPERIENCE:
The kind of experience any woman gets when dating
Packwood, Bob or Kennedy, Ted.

HARRELSON, WOODY:
Liberal TV and film actor who rushed to protest the
Gulf War as another Vietnam. Called "Woody"
because he has the head of a three-wood.

HART, GARY:
Former senator (D-CO) who lusted for the presidency
but screwed himself out of it.

HARVARD:
Kremlin on the Charles. "I'd rather entrust the government of the United States to the first four hundred
people listed in the Boston telephone directory than to
the faculty of Harvard."
—*William F. Buckley, Jr.*

HATE SPEECH:
What liberals say to incite the media into quoting
them. Examples:
a) "I hope [Supreme Court Justice Clarence Thomas's]
   wife feeds him lots of butter and he dies early like
   many black men do, of heart disease.... He is absolutely reprehensible."
   —*Julianne Malveaux on PBS' "To the Contrary"*

b) "[Newt Gingrich] is one of the most dangerous figures to emerge in American politics during our lifetime.... He calls himself a revolutionary, but he promotes the policies of a terrorist."

—*Congressman Martin Frost (D-TX) in a Democratic Congressional Campaign Committee fundraising letter*

c) "The Christian Coalition was a strong force in Germany. It laid down a suitable, scientific, theological rationale for the tragedy in Germany. The Christian Coalition was very much in evidence there."

—*Jesse Jackson in USA Today*

d) "Imagine the monstrous consequences if Newt succeeds in making starvation public policy in a society where the poor are heavily armed."

—*Myrlie Evers-Williams, chairwoman of the NAACP*

e) "[Militia members are] angry white men...sort of in their natural state. This is the essence of the angry white man...."

—*Juan Williams on Capital Gang*

f) "Where once we had the sheets and hoods of the KKK, now we have the black suits and red ties of conservative politicians. It's not 'spics and niggers' anymore; it's 'let's cut taxes.'"

—*Congressman Charles Rangel (D-NY)*

g) "[Oliver North is] raising money from the extreme right—the extra-chromosome right."

> —*Vice President Al Gore*

h) "[Newt Gingrich and the Republicans are] reptilian bastards."

> —*George Bushneil, president of the American Bar Association*

HAUTE COUTURE:
Fashion so rude it had to be given a French name.

HEARTLAND:
Wherever nonacademic, non-liberal, real Americans live. "The Republicans have become the party of the heartland. The Democrats have become the party of Washington, of the bureaucracy."

> —*Chicago Mayor Richard Daley, Jr.*

(Which explains why Chicago voters are turning over in their graves to reregister.) Because of their proposals for higher taxes, more government spending, and more regulation, the Democrats have become the party of heartattackland.

HELIUM RESERVE:
1) Often-cited example of a useless federal program.
2) During Senate filibusters, Robert Byrd's second wind.

HELL:

Liberal utopian society where there is no religious right, no family values, no traditional morality, no mixing of church and state, and no prayer in school, or anywhere else for that matter.

"HE'S NOT CRAZY ANYMORE":

Campaign slogan proposed by Richard Malmed for New York senatorial candidate Al Sharpton, who was trying to moderate his image.

HETEROSEXUAL:

A traditional sexual orientation reportedly coming back into fashion...so don't throw out your old wardrobe quite yet.

HILL, ANITA:

Liberal feminist professor who testified against Clarence Thomas's nomination to the U.S. Supreme Court. Suspicions were raised when she swore to tell the half-truth, and nothing like the truth, then revealed that her name was originally Anita Molehill.

HISS, ALGER:

U.S. State Department official, noted liberal, and accused traitor convicted of perjury, who regretted that he had but one country to give for his life.

HISTORY:

(1) Something liberals like to rewrite to prove they're always right. (2) "A race between education and catastrophe."

—H. G. Wells

Today, they're pretty much the same thing.

HIT FOR THE CYCLE:

In baseball, when a batter has a single, double, triple, and home run in one game. *Note*: Do not confuse this expression with "a hit for the psycho," which refers to any profitable film directed by Oliver Stone.

HOLLINGS, ERNEST:

Slow-talking, even slower thinking senator (D-SC), who makes observers wonder, "What did he know, and will he ever know it?"

HOLLYWOOD:

A place where movie people live and work between stays at the Betty Ford Clinic.

HOMELESSNESS:

The only sure way to avoid high property taxes.

HOMOPHOBIA:

What you're guilty of if you ever pointed out that congressmen Barney Frank and Gerry Studds represent abutting districts.

HONESTLY:

Word used by politicians to signal an upcoming lie.

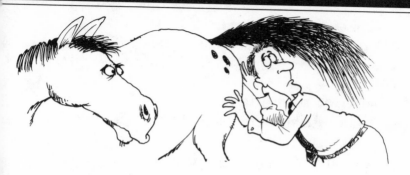

HORSE'S MOUTH:

A reliable source, as in the expression, "I heard it right from the horse's mouth." Conversely, anything coming from Democratic consultant James Carville is said to be "straight from the horse's ass."

HOWARD, SHEMP:

Deceased actor who played one of the Three Stooges, and claimed recently as a "distant relation" by Congressman Barney Frank. Sure, now that Shemp can't sue for defamation of character.

HUGGING:

The sensitive liberal's hello.

HUMANISM:

Belief that man's soul is found only in African-American music.

HUMANITARIANISM:
"Almost always a false front for the urge to rule."
—*H. L. Mencken*

HUMAN SERVICES:
Phrase used to describe social workers and other bureaucrats who resist *self*-service. Their credo was inspired by C. G. Jung: "Show me a sane man and I will cure him for you."

HUNTING:
The pursuit and killing of game. Many elitists deplore hunting, but if they disapprove of it, why do gourmet restaurants keep serving duck, pheasant, and venison?

HUSSEIN, SADDAM:
The real Thief of Baghdad; give him an inch and he'll take a country.

ICELAND:
Home of the world's oldest functioning democracy,
which has survived for centuries despite spending little
for defense because who the hell wants Iceland anyway?

IDEALISM:
Liberals' favorite excuse for their failures.

IDEAS HAVE CONSEQUENCES:
(1) Title of prophetic book of the 1950s by a brilliant conservative, Richard Weaver. (2) Epitaph for '90s liberalism.

ILLITERATE:
An anti-semantic.

IMPULSE CONTROL DISORDER:
Controversial legal defense theory that criminals
shouldn't be held responsible for their actions because
they are unable to control their fundamental urges—a
theory universally applauded by teenage boys.

INAPPROPRIATE:
Contemporary synonym for "bad," "evil," or "immoral."
For example, "It was inappropriate for the Menendez
boys to blow their parents' heads off with a shotgun."

INCLUSION:

To be taken in as part of the whole. For liberals, this includes "everybody but white males and conservatives."

—*Rush Limbaugh*

Under affirmative action, however, liberals do favor putting white males *in* a hole.

INCONGRUOUS:

"Where our laws are made." —*Bennett Cerf*

INDEPENDENCE:

Core value of conservatism. "The proverb warns you that you should not bite the hand that feeds you. But maybe you should, if it prevents you from feeding yourself."

—*Thomas Szasz*

INDEPENDENTS:

Voters not satisfied with choosing between two evils. They'd prefer to have three or four.

INDIGNATION:

The other nation (*See* Alienation) that liberals feel patriotic about.

INFLATION:

A sneaky pay cut.

INTELLECTUAL:

Someone who can listen to the *William Tell Overture* without thinking about the Lone Ranger.

INTELLIGENTSIA:

(1) Polite way to say, "It's those damn liberals again!"
(2) Part-time intellectuals often seen at foreign movies.

INTERACTIVE TV:

Futuristic TV in which the viewer and the TV interact with each other. It already exists in a primitive form now because not only can viewers turn the TV on, but modern TV also turns many viewers off.

INTERNET:

Complex, worldwide web of connected computers that enables an individual to access information on just about anything. It's what your teenage son is using right now to ogle naked women.

INTROSPECTION:

Trying to change the diapers of your inner child.

INVENTION:

"Build a better mousetrap, and the government will build a better mousetrap tax."

—Lawrence J. Peter

IRELAND, NORTHERN:

"Anyone who isn't confused here doesn't really understand what is going on."

—Belfast resident

Ditto for Washington, D.C.

IRELAND, PATRICIA:
President of the National Organization for Women, who proved she was liberated by leaving her husband for a woman and then refusing to take the woman's last name.

JAPAN:
A country that exports Sonys and Toyotas in wholesale quantities and charges its own people $31.00 for a cherry. Some economists think we ought to emulate their economy...except for that cherry thing.

JOBS PROGRAM:
"When Bill Clinton said he'd create millions of new jobs, no one realized he meant for special prosecutors."

—National Review

JONES, PAULA:
Bill Clinton's idea of room service.

JULIUS:
A name Hillary Clinton called her first car. The car called her a bitch.

JUST DO IT:
Nike's advertising slogan.

JUST DONE IT:
Ted Kennedy's slogan.

JUVENILE DELINQUENT:
In the 1950s, someone who smacked gum in class, carried smokes, and drove a motorcycle. Today, someone who smacks the teacher in class, carries a smoking gun, and drives a getaway car.

K

KEILLOR, GARRISON:
National Public Radio's idea of a humorist. An NPR executive defended the radio network's judgment by pointing out that on 14 June 1987, a listener in Omaha,

Nebraska, actually chuckled during a broadcast of *A Prairie Home Companion.*

KENNEDY, JOHN F.:
(1) Thirty-fifth president of the United States; idolized by liberals for having glamorized politics, but conservative on every issue by today's standards, if you don't count marital fidelity. (2) One of the few Kennedys not caught during his lifetime.

KENNEDY, JOHN, JR.:
Son of the former president. Unlike Uncle Ted, he made the mistake of taking his own exams.

KENNEDY, JOSEPH III:
Short...uh...tempered and...uh Democratic...uh ...congressman from...uh...Massachusetts...who can never... uh... get...uh...a...uh...clear and... uh...coherent ...um...thought out of...um...his mouth...because he...um...doesn't have...um... one in...um...his head.

KENNEDY, TED:
The funniest damned politician in America.

KERRY, JOHN F.:
Liberal Democratic senator from Massachusetts, also known as "an empty suit of clothes," as reported by

the *Wall Street Journal*. His wardrobe has improved noticeably since marrying the heiress of the $650 million Heinz fortune; the couple is known in D.C. as Cash and Kerry.

KHADDAFI, MUAMMAR (ALSO KA-DAFFY):
Libyan dictator and nutcase who often says he is prepared to die for his beliefs. Most people are willing to let him.

KHOMEINI, AYATOLLAH:
Deceased dictator of Iran who proved that even fanaticism could be overdone.

KICK-OFF:
(1) Announcement of a candidacy or launching of a campaign. (2) What Bill Clinton did with his pants to impress Paula Jones.

KING, DON:
An ego on steroids.

KING, LARRY:
Much-married talk show host who would be far better off if, once in a while, he loved and lost.

KING, RODNEY:
Man awarded millions after being beaten by Los Angeles police during a drunk driving arrest. When King heard about his windfall, he said, "I'll drink to that," and reportedly hasn't stopped since.

KING, STEPHEN:
Best-selling author of horror stories, including *The Stand, Pet Sematary, Cujo,* and *The Clinton Years.*

KISSINGER, HENRY:
Former secretary of state under Presidents Nixon and Ford. After former Secretary of Defense Robert S. McNamara confessed errors of judgment about

Vietnam, Kissinger admitted that he himself had never been wrong about anything.

KITCHEN CABINET:
(1) A politician's inner circle of informal advisers.
(2) Where failed Clinton nominees Zoe Baird and Kimba Wood hid their illegal immigrant housekeepers when the FBI dropped by to ask if they had any skeletons in their closets.

KNOW-NOTHING PARTY:
The raucous celebrating of selected jurors, overjoyed at having made the cut.

KUNTSLER, WILLIAM:
Longtime left-wing lawyer who was known for defending criminal extremists and extreme criminals.

L

LAW SCHOOL:

Course of study described as extremely difficult, but apparently not difficult enough to stop 800,000 predators from becoming lawyers.

LAWYERS:

Rats with briefcases. Many people mistakenly think the line by Shakespeare, "The first thing we do, let's kill all the lawyers," is one of the Ten Commandments.

LEADERSHIP:

In politics, the art of persuading people to support a set of ideas or policies, after first checking the polls to make certain that you are only persuading them to believe what they already believe. Amazingly, many politicians still fail at this.

LECTOR, HANNIBAL/DAHMER, JEFFREY:
Fictional and nonfictional characters who devoured the dead. Compare to: *Internal Revenue Service,* which devours the living.

LENIENCY:
A liberal willingness to forgive and forget crimes committed against someone else.

LIABILITY (LIE-ABILITY):
The contemporary notion that if you are injured, no matter how careless you were and no matter how personally responsible you were for your injury, you are still entitled to sue anyone who has a bank account.

LIBERAL:
One who doesn't care how many people have to lose their money and freedom in order to make this a caring, unselfish world.

LIBERALISM:
The sin that dare not speak its name to voters. It always campaigns under an alias, such as "moderate"

or "progressive." P. J. O'Rourke defines liberalism as the philosophy of "sniveling brats," although fair-minded folk consider this unfair to sniveling brats.

LIBERAL DEMOCRAT:
A politician whose future is past.

LIBERAL INTELLECTUAL:
Someone who thinks too much for our own good.

LIBERAL JUSTICE:
A trial where they lock up the jurors and let the defendant go free.

LIE DETECTOR TEST:
Method to determine whether a person is lying by measuring respiration, galvanic skin response, and

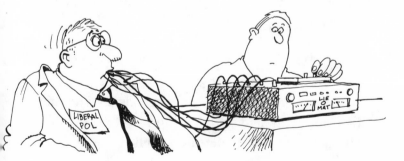

other bodily functions. Or, in the case of a liberal politician, just check to see if the subject's lips are moving.

LIFE ISN'T FAIR:
(1) What President Kennedy tried explaining to liberals instead of saying, "Grow up!" (2) What Ted Kennedy proved in a courtroom.

LIFESTYLE:
What Yuppies set out to acquire when told, "Get a life!"

LIMBAUGH, RUSH:
Conservative radio and TV talk show host. Known to his fans as the Traffic Cop of Common Sense; known to liberals as Tyrannosaurus Rush.

LITIGIOUS SOCIETY:
What a country turns into when it ends up with more than half of all lawyers in the world—800,000—all willing to sue you if you call them litigious.

LITTLE ROCK:

Capital of Arkansas, located in the center of the state, and surrounded by graft and chicken droppings.

LIVE FREE OR DIE:

New Hampshire's motto. Not to be confused with the motto of New Hampshire welfare recipients: "We're dying to live free."

LOOPHOLE:

To liberals, any provision of the tax code that fails to claim money earned, inherited, saved, or otherwise pocketed by known taxpayers.

LOOTING:

Window-shopping by the underprivileged.

LOS ANGELES:
"The City of Angels," Lucifer in particular.

LOSING:
"The great American sin."

—*John Tunis*

LOSING TO A LIBERAL:
The great American embarrassment.

LSD:
(1) Liberal Senate Democrat. (2) Lysergic acid diethylamide, a psychotropic drug that can cause psychotic symptoms, such as hallucinations, severe depression, and thoughts of suicide. Curiously, watching the evening news can cause the same symptoms.

LUNATIC FRINGE:
Congressman David Bonior's beard.

LYIN' KING:
Proposed animated version of Bill Clinton's biography.

M

MACHIAVELLIAN:
Political cunning and duplicity. Contrary to widespread belief, Bill Clinton is *not* Machiavellian. Instead of following Machiavelli's advice that "cruelties should be committed all at once," Clinton decided to spread them over four years, on the theory that if you cut a cat's tail one inch at a time, it will hurt less.

MADONNA:
In the words of Mae West, the kind of girl who climbed the ladder of success wrong by wrong.

MAFIA:
A term Bill Clinton used to describe former New York governor Mario Cuomo in a telephone conversation with, and secretly taped by, Gennifer Flowers. Clinton claimed he never said it, but apologized to Cuomo on behalf of the voice that sounded like his.

MALAISE:
A vague sense of ill-being or loss of faith. Jimmy Carter cited it when he discovered that Americans had

lost faith in *him.* Bill Clinton discovered the same malady in Americans during his first term, but his staff talked him out of using the word because he kept pronouncing it, "my lays."

MALCONTENT:
Someone who always wants what he doesn't have. The problem is, what else can you want?

MANDATE:
(1) What Democrats argue Clinton got in 1992 with 43 percent of the vote, but what Republicans failed to get in 1994 when they won 53 percent of Congressional seats. (2) Something no radical feminist has on Saturday night.

MANHATTAN SOCIALITE:
Someone who practices designer politics.

MANKIND:
Politically incorrect term for personkind, or better still, personsofallcolorkind—or, for special occasions, personsofallcolorethnicheritagereligionsandsexual-preferencekind.

MANSON, CHARLES:
Head of an extremely dysfunctional family.

MAPPLETHORPE, ROBERT:
Deceased photographer known for pictures of sado-masochism, depravity, and vulgarity. Liberals defend his work on the grounds that his photos are so offensive they must be considered true art.

MARRIAGE PENALTY:
(1) A term referring to the fact that a married couple pays much higher taxes than two people cohabitating without marriage. (2) Being married to Hillary or Bill.

MARTYR:
A true believer who gets carried away—by pallbearers.

MARX, KARL:
The Marx brother who chose tragedy over comedy.

MASON, C. VERNON:
Political activist who defended Mike Tyson after Tyson's release from prison, arguing, "Hear about the woman in South Carolina who drove her children into the river and drowned them? Mike Tyson didn't do that.... Hear about the bomb that was dropped on the building in Oklahoma City? Mike Tyson didn't do that. Do you all remember Jeffrey Dahmer, who ate all the people and put them in a refrigerator? Mike Tyson

didn't do that." *Hear about Desiree Washington, the beauty contestant who was brutally raped? Mike Tyson did that.*

MASS TRANSIT:
Any form of public transportation that involves moving many people simultaneously. Most fiercely advocated by those who wouldn't be caught dead using it.

MASTIGOPHORAN:
A class of protozoans that have flagella. (Just checking to see if you're paying attention.)

MATALIN, MARY:
Conservative TV talk show host and former political operative for President Bush. She was so devastated by her candidate's loss that she married Clinton strategist James Carville as penance. At least that's one explanation. The other is that she married him for the pleasure of eventually divorcing him.

McCARTHY, EUGENE:
Former Democratic senator who challenged incumbent president Lyndon Johnson in the primaries. When fellow Democrats charged that he was dividing the

party, McCarthy asked, "Have you ever tried to split sawdust?"

McCARTHYISM:

Political repression now practiced in Russia by voters who ask candidates, "Are you now, or have you ever been, a member of the Communist Party?"

McGOVERN, GEORGE:

(1) Unsuccessful presidential nominee in 1972. After losing, he said: "We opened the doors of the Democratic Party as we promised we would, and twenty million Democrats stalked out."

(2) A politician whose foreign policy was based on two key principles: begging and groveling.

MEAN-SPIRITED:

Calling a liberal Democratic incumbent politician vicious, degrading names like liberal, Democratic, incumbent, politician.

MEDIA BIAS:

A redundancy. "There's no such thing as objective reporting," a *Boston Globe* reporter was quoted as saying at a liberal conclave. "I've become even more crafty about finding the voices to say the things I think are true. That's my subversive mission." After her comments were reported, she was reprimanded with a stern promotion.

MEDIA CIRCUS:
A news spectacle that has gotten so out of control that reporters spend almost as much time deploring it as they do enjoying it.

MEMORY:
What liberals don't want to clutter up with a lot of facts, experience, and reality.

MEXICAN BAILOUT:
Billions given to Mexico by the United States, reasoning that if we don't lend them the money, they won't pay us back what they already owe us.

MIDDLE CLASS:
What 95 percent of Americans proudly and insistently call themselves, while buying lottery tickets to escape it.

MIDNIGHT BASKETBALL:
Liberal program to lower the crime rate between midnight and 2:00 A.M. twice a week.

MIRANDA RIGHTS:
What the Supreme Court ruled must be read by arresting officers to criminal suspects. These include: the right to be represented by a free court-appointed

lawyer, the right to be freed on a technicality by a liberal judge, the right to be exonerated by an ignorant jury, the right to become a celebrity from irresponsible media coverage, the right to have color TV in prison, the right to sue the prison for bad cooking, the right to early parole if you can't break out of prison, the right to a well-stocked prison law library so you can draft endless frivolous appeals, and the right to a decent book deal to tell how you have always been mistreated.

MOMMY:
"What President Ronald Reagan called his wife, Nancy. President Bill Clinton calls his wife Sir."
—*Alex Beam and Jeff Danziger*

MONDALE, WALTER:
Another unsuccessful liberal nominee for president. "Mr. Mondale has said that God doesn't belong in

politics, and apparently God feels the same way about Mr. Mondale."

—*Mark Russell*

MONEY:
It is often mistakenly said that "money is the root of all evil." The actual quote is, "The *love* of money is the root of all evil." Both are wrong. As R. Emmett Tyrell points out, "Evil is the root of all evil."

MORAL COMPASS:
A guiding device needed by any politician pretending to be a Boy Scout.

MORAL EDUCATION:
What the teachers' union says has no place in public schools. Considering the condition of most public schools, they're right.

MORAL INDIGNATION:
"Jealousy with a halo."

—*H. G. Wells*

MORALITY:
(1) "Drawing the line somewhere."

—*G. K. Chesterton*

(2) If imposed by conservatives: bad. If imposed by

liberals: good. If imposed by the mass media: movie-of-the-week.

MORAL RELATIVISM:
A term that's never been applied to Roger Clinton.

MOTHER OF ALL BATTLES:
Phrase used by Saddam Hussein to describe the climactic battle he intended to wage against U.S. forces in the Gulf War. "Yours is a society which cannot accept 10,000 dead in one battle," Saddam claimed. He was right, so the United States chose to administer the "Mother of All Thrashings" instead.

MOYERS, BILL:
Liberal TV commentator who often goes too far. If only he'd stay there.

MTV:
Massaging Teen Vanities.

MUDSLINGING:
When candidates share their true feelings with each other.

MULTICULTURALISM:
Course of studies denigrating Western civilization, while exalting primitive societies, e.g., the proposition

that Leonardo da Vinci and Abraham Lincoln had much to learn from cannibals.

MURDER:
What Hillary Clinton got away with in her commodities trading.

NAKED GUY:
Nickname for student at University of California, Berkeley, who insisted on attending classes naked. Eventually suspended by Berkeley authorities on the grounds that he was barely acceptable...or rather, he wasn't.

NANNY COMPLEX:
Government-knows-best philosophy that seeks to protect consumers against *any* risk. Example: mandatory warnings about high cholesterol on cheese-baited mousetraps.

NASA:

National Aeronautics and Space Administration, the
U.S. space agency that designed and built the largest
rocket ever, the Saturn V. To give some idea of the
awesome power of the Saturn V, it generated almost
enough thrust to lift Ted Kennedy off a barroom floor.

NATIONAL CONDOM WEEK:

Another attempted government cover-up.

NATIONAL COUNCIL OF CHURCHES:

An association of liberal congregations prepared to
endorse any nonsense so long as it isn't mentioned or
prescribed in the Bible.

NATIONAL DEBT:

The total sum owed by *future* Americans to *current*
banks, arranged by *past* politicians.

NATIONAL ORGANIZATION FOR WOMEN (N.O.W.):

Left-wing group that N.E.V.E.R. speaks for a majority
of women.

NATIVE AMERICANS:

Asian migrants who came to America across an
ancient land bridge and proceeded to dispossess,

exploit, and slaughter the true native Americans—
buffalo and prairie weasels.

NATURE:

A term used in an awed tone by ecologists because
they believe that all of nature is innately wise—except,
of course, human nature. Liberals find the term
"Mother Nature" politically incorrect because it
implies that tornadoes, hurricanes, earthquakes, tidal
waves, pestilence, and the Ebola virus should be
blamed on a metaphysical femme fatale.

NC-17:

Movie rating given to films so depraved that No
Conservative over seventeen should be admitted.

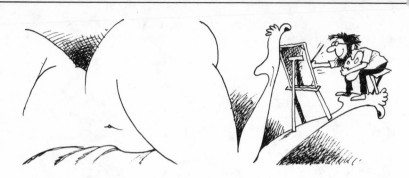

NEA:
National Endowment for the Arts, the group that funds artists who often display just how well endowed they are.

NEED:
A liberal's favorite four-letter word.

NEGATIVE ADVERTISING:
Something the voting public hates to love.

NEOCONSERVATIVE:
A liberal Democrat up for reelection.

NEW AGE:
Communing, chants, crystal, chromium, and other con artistry.

NEW AGE MUSIC:
Middlebrow melodies for the middle-aged of
Aquarius.

NEW COVENANT:
Phrase taken from the Bible by Bill Clinton to describe
his political agenda. Some biblical scholars feel that he
overlooked more suitable themes for his administration:

"I know...the naughtiness of thine heart."
—1 Samuel 17:28

"The way of a fool is right in his own eyes."
—Proverbs 12:15

"He multiplieth words without knowledge."
—Job 35:16

"Where there is no vision, the people perish."
—Proverbs 29:18

"How long hold ye between two opinions?"
—1 Kings 18:21

"The companion of fools shall be destroyed."
—Proverbs 13:20

"The last error shall be worse than the first."
—Matthew 27:64

"And he girded up his loins."
—1 Kings 18:46

NEW DEMOCRAT:
Term that reporters mistakenly thought Bill Clinton used to describe himself in the 1992 campaign. He actually said *nude* Democrat.

NEWS HOUR WITH JIM LEHRER :
PBS test for attention deficit disorder.

NEW WORLD ORDER:
Same Old Disorder.

NEW YORK CITY:
(1) The city that never sleeps—too many sirens. (2) A city where residents have 911 on automatic speed-dial.

NIGHT OF THE LIVING DEAD:
For Democratic incumbents, the first Tuesday evening in November, 1994.

NONPARTISAN:
Media euphemism for a liberal special interest group.

NORTON, ELEANOR HOLMES:
Former head of the Civil Rights Commission, later elected Washington, D.C.'s nonvoting representative to Congress even though she failed to pay city taxes for

eight years. A clear case of "representation without taxation."

—*Mark Shields*

"NOT TO WORRY":
Contemporary phrase of reassurance. It means: Worry.

NOVAK, ROBERT:
Conservative columnist and TV personality. Liberals call him the "Prince of Darkness." As usual, they've got it wrong: He's the *King* of Darkness.

NRA:
National Rifle Association. Outspoken defender of the Second Amendment to the Constitution, the right to bear arms and scare liberals. Its unofficial slogan was first uttered by Steve McQueen in the movie *The Magnificent Seven:* "We deal in lead."

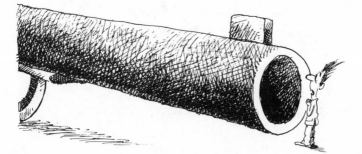

NUCLEAR POWER:
An energy source created by God to annoy Martin Sheen.

NUNN, SAM:
Moderate senator (D-GA) who decided against running for Vice President with Michael Dukakis when the Massachusetts liberal rejected his idea for a campaign slogan: "Vote for Nunn and the above."

NURTURE/NATURE DEBATE:
An argument among sensitive liberals over whether you should learn to hug your inner child before you hug a tree.

OBJECTIVE:
How biased journalists describe their reporting because they have a clear, simple objective: Destroy conservativism.

O'CONNOR, SINEAD:
Sometimes-bald feminist singer who tore up a picture of the Pope on *Saturday Night Live* and once said, "Hitler wasn't a bad person; he was a very screwed-up person." Sinead isn't a bad singer...

OFFICE OF SOLID WASTE MANAGEMENT:
Unofficial title for the office of White House Chief of Staff Leon Panetta.

OFF-SHORE DRILLING:
What Howell Heflin thought he saw Ted Kennedy doing in a sailboat.

OMNIVEROUS:
Descriptive of an organism that will devour anything, e.g., The Federal Government.

ONO, YOKO:
Another example of the U.S. trade deficit with Japan.

ORPHANAGE:
Term used by Newt Gingrich that outraged liberals. He should have said "twenty-four-hour day care."

OUTWEEK:

Gay magazine whose staff "outed" prominent homosexuals and also opposed Robert Bork's appointment to the Supreme Court because they believed he threatened the right to privacy.

OVAL OFFICE:

Given its current occupant, yet more proof that it's hard to put a blockhead in a round hole.

P

PACKWOOD DEFENSE:

"I wasn't kissing her, I was whispering in her mouth."
—*Chico Marx*

PAIN:

What Bill Clinton says he feels in people, probably because he causes so much of it.

PARANOIA:

A belief that people despise you and are talking against you. In Bill Clinton's case, it's called polling.

PARENTAL CHOICE:
The PC that liberals *don't* want to see in public schools.

PARENTING:
"A class that liberals argue should be taught in public school, preferably in junior high, in case the banana lesson, self-esteem class, and sex education don't work."

—*Debra J. Saunders*

PAROLE:
System to release violent criminals before they've served their full sentences in order to reduce the surplus population of innocent people.

PBS:
(1) The great unwatched. (2) *P* stands for *Public*, which means government funding. Everyone knows what the BS stands for.

PEACE THROUGH STRENGTH:
Conservative defense philosophy summed up by Josh Billings: "There may come a time when the lion and the lamb will lie down together, but I am still betting on the lion." This is because the lion will be at peace, while the lamb will be in pieces.

PEROT, ROSS:

A multibillionaire simpleton who likes to alternate between giving democracy a bad name and giving capitalism a bad name.

"PERSON OF THE WEEK":

ABC weekly news segment that focuses on an individual who reportedly has "made a difference" that particular week. Since these are nearly always establishment liberals, the network might rename the segment "Person of the Weak."

PETA:

People for the Ethical Treatment of Animals, an organization opposed to steak.

PETRIFIED FOREST:

Al Gore's hometown.

PHILLIPS, KEVIN:

Favorite "Republican" analyst for network news shows because he's always arguing that Republicans will never be successful unless they become more like Democrats. After the results of the 1994 elections, Phillips argued that it was time to select a new electorate.

PHONE SEX:
The previously undiscovered constitutional right of the socially impaired to reach out and touch someone.

PISTACHIO:
Only nut not appointed to a job in the Clinton administration.

PLATFORM:
Set of principles candidates stand on, usually to crush them.

PLURALISM:
"Two or more liberal views."

—*Rush Limbaugh*

POCAHONTAS:
(1) Female Native American who befriended the Pilgrims and taught them how to plant corn. (2) Title of Disney Company's politically correct movie that criticizes man's exploitation of the natural land. This does *not* apply to corporations that build theme parks on undeveloped land in California, Florida, Japan, or France.

POLARIZING:
What liberals claim conservatives are doing when they fight for something favored by 80 percent in the polls.

POLITENESS:
"Art of selecting among one's real thoughts."
— *Madame de Staël*

POLITICAL BUZZ-SAW WORDS:
A list compiled by GOPAC, a Republican campaign group, and sent to GOP candidates to help them define the terms of debate with their opponents. Among the words suggested to describe Democratic positions were: *decay, failure, collapse, welfare, radical, taxes, spending, criminal rights* ... Liberals charged GOPAC with plagiarism for stealing the text of the next Democratic platform.

POLITICAL CORRECTNESS (PC):
Insensitive persecution of people accused of being insensitive by liberals insensitive enough to think of themselves as terribly sensitive.

POLITICAL CREDIBILITY:
When a politician can get voters to suspend their disbelief.

POLITICAL PHILOSOPHY:

The study of the ideas behind major historical movements. In America, these movements are often associated with specific historical figures, e.g., federalism/Alexander Hamilton; republicanism/ Abraham Lincoln; hedonism/Ted Kennedy.

POLITICAL SCIENCE/SOCIOLOGY:

Unscientific politics and politicized science.

POLITICIAN:

"A man who can be verbose in fewer words than anyone else."

—Peter de Vries

POLLING:

Sampling the opinions of five hundred people who aren't smart enough to hang up on a pollster.

POSNER, VLADIMIR:

Former apologist for the former Soviet Union and its former leaders. He now has a talk show with cohost Phil Donahue, on which Posner's socialist philosophy serves as the conservative counterfoil to Donahue's views.

POST OFFICE:
Headquarters of the largest known terrorist group in the United States: disgruntled workers.

POVERTY PROGRAMS:
Bureaucracy set up to help poor people. The programs are very expensive, but we do get a lot of poverty for our money.

PRAGMATISM:
A willingness to be flexible, exemplified by Richard Nixon's statement, "I'll speak for the candidate, or against him, whichever will do him the most good."

PRESIDENTIAL DIET:
Bill Clinton's resolution to just *tell* Whoppers.

PRESS:
A term that refers to newspapers. "Everything you read in the newspaper is absolutely true except for the rare story of which you happen to have firsthand knowledge."

—*Erwin Knoll*

PRESS SECRETARY:
A kind of zookeeper who knows that if he doesn't feed the beasts, he'll get eaten by them.

PRIVATE SECTOR:
To liberals, a jungle where animals roam free and must scramble to feed themselves, in contrast to the public sector, where animals roam the bureaucratic zoo feasting on taxpayers.

PROFESSIONAL POLITICIANS:
People who don't run for public office—they stampede for it.

PROGRESS:
Until 1994, the opposite of *Con*gress.

PROGRESSIVE:
Kinder, gentler way of saying radical.

PROPERTY RIGHTS:
"Communism doesn't work because people like to own stuff."

—*Frank Zappa*

PROPOSITION 187:
California referendum aimed at discouraging illegal immigration and based on the advice of a Native American to Lyndon Johnson: "Be careful with your immigration laws. We were careless with ours."

PROSPERITY:
Economic growth resented by left-wing ideologues because it is enjoyed by the prospering.

PROZAC:
A drug that makes you happy that you're depressed. Developed just in time for the Clinton era.

PSYCHIATRY:
"Care of the id by the odd."

—Anonymous

PSYCHOBABBLE:
Second language of Northern California.

PUBLIC SERVANT:
How incumbent politicians describe themselves, even though a servant is far more likely to wax your car

than tax your car, and far more likely to clean your
house than clean you out.

PUNDITS:
Opinion-mongers.

PURSUIT OF HAPPINESS:
"The Declaration of Independence says, We are
endowed by our Creator with certain unalienable
rights, among which are life, liberty, and the pursuit of
happiness. It talks about the right of the *pursuit* of
happiness. There's no reference to happiness stamps—
to a happiness entitlement, to happiness therapy, to
happiness victimization."

—Newt Gingrich

QUEER NATION:
A radical gay rights group demanding liberation from
people who call them queer.

R

RADICAL FEMINIST:
A woman who is way too fond of women.

RAINBOW COALITION:
Jesse Jackson's political organization, reflecting the fact that a rainbow has every color of the spectrum, except white.

RAP MUSIC:
(1) Rhythm without melody, rhyme without reason.
(2) Called "rap" because listeners often want to rap the singer upside the head with a two-by-four to shut him up.

RATHER, DAN:
Rather liberal, Rather biased, Rather strange.

REAGANOMICS:
Longest peacetime economic expansion in U.S. history. Called a recession by Democrats in Congress because their influence dramatically receded.

REAGAN, RONALD:

"Not a typical politician because he doesn't know how to lie, cheat, and steal. He's always had an agent for that."

—Bob Hope

REAL WORLD:

What liberals will discuss but never visit.

REFORMER:

Someone who constantly preaches in favor of various kinds of reform: education reform, health care reform, campaign finance reform…causing everyone else to pray for chloroform.

REGULATOR:

Government official who wants to mind your own business.

REHABILITATION:

What criminals pretend to undergo once they discover that crime is much easier to commit outside of prison.

REINVENTING GOVERNMENT:

Title of Vice President Al Gore's book on making government more "businesslike." It cost the Government

Printing Office more than three times the normal cost of a government book.

RELIGIOUS LEFT:

A term banned by the mass media, where most have left religion. To liberal reporters and commentators, there is no such thing as a religious left, even though Jesse Jackson, Al Sharpton, the National Council of Churches, and others like them haul out their starched collars when declaiming the moral high ground on the network news.

RENO, JANET:

Attorney general of the United States and Bill Clinton's father figure.

RENT CONTROL:

A system that turns landlords into serfs so that liberal tenants can avoid the high rents that liberal policies force everyone else to pay. (North Vietnam lifted rent control after the war, explained Hanoi's Finance Minister, because it did more damage than U.S. bombing.)

REPUBLICAN:

Political philosophy based on the idea that work is therapy, and if you work hard enough, anything is possible. Compare to *Democrat:* A political philosophy that the harder you work, the more you need therapy.

RESTRAINING ORDER:
What the voters issued against Bill Clinton and the Democrats in the 1994 elections.

REVELATIONS:
How conservatives refer to the *Wall Street Journal* editorial page.

RICH:
To liberals, anyone who makes a living without government aid.

ROBIN HOOD:
Legendary character admired by liberals not because he took from the rich to give to the poor but because

he hung around with merry men in a conservation area and refused to get a real job.

ROCKEFELLER, JAY:
Absurdly rich and liberal U.S. senator (D-WV) who proves the old saying that a fool and his money are soon elected.

ROGUE'S SCHOLAR:
Bill Clinton's new endowment for White House interns.

ROLLING STONE:
Magazine covering rock music. "People who can't write interviewing people who can't talk for people who can't read."

—*Frank Zappa*

ROWAN, CARL:
Columnist and vigorous proponent of gun control, who once shot a teenager for using his swimming pool. When accused of using a gun to wound the youth, Rowan explained that he merely held the bullet in his teeth while his wife whacked him in back of the head with a sledgehammer.

ROYAL FLUSH:
Prince Charles's reaction after reading the transcripts
of his phone calls to Camilla Parker-Bowles.

RULING CLASS:
Something the British royal family could use a lot
more of.

RUSSIA:
A nation of badly dressed alcoholics with nuclear
weapons.

S

SACRIFICE:
Liberal euphemism for a tax hike on the middle class.

SAFE SEX:
Refusing to date anyone named Kennedy.

SAFER SEX:
Marrying Michael Jackson.

SAFETY NET:
Hundreds of federal programs carefully woven together to ensure that no social worker falls into the private sector.

SARANDON, SUSAN AND ROBBINS, TIM:
Cohabitating actress and actor who cover their bodies with colored ribbons during Academy Award appearances to show that they are all wrapped up in themselves.

SARCASM:
What liberal journalists call conservative humor; liberal humor is called wit, irony, or satire.

SAVE THE WHALES:

A primary goal of Greenpeace and a worthy aim, but how do you deposit one to your account?

SAVING:

Accumulating assets. "A very fine thing, especially when your parents have done it for you."

—*Winston Churchill*

SAXOPHONE:

The instrument Bill Clinton plays with—well, one of them.

SCARS:

What Al Gore's dermatologist discovered were really woodpecker marks.

SCHOOL VOUCHERS:

A system that allows parents to choose where to send their children to school. Opposed by teachers' unions out of fear that parents might use learning as a standard for choosing.

SCHROEDER, PATRICIA:

Liberal congresswoman (D-CO) with a mouth that won't quit and a personality that won't start. Her staff regularly puts out press releases highlighting her near-life experiences.

SEND IN THE CLOWNS:

The message given to the House doorkeeper when Congress is ready to receive Bill Clinton and his entourage for the State of the Union address.

SENSITIVITY TRAINING:
Learning to stay awake while other people whine.

SENTIMENTALITY:
"What we call the sentiment we don't share."

—Graham Greene

SEVEN DEADLY SINS:
Pride, covetousness, lust, anger, gluttony, sloth, and envy—civil rights to modern-day liberals.

SHRIVER, MARIA:
TV news-magazine interviewer. Although a member of the Kennedy family, there's not one bad thing to say about her—because she's married to Arnold Schwarzenegger, an immense, muscular Republican who can whack the hell out of anyone who insults his wife.

SIMON, PAUL:
Nerdy liberal senator.

SIMON, PAUL:
Nerdy liberal singer.

SIMPLE SIMON:
See Simon, Paul.

SIMPSON TRIAL:
A TV show about Broncos, Itos, Katos, Yo-yos, and Bozos.

SITUATION ETHICS:
Feel good now, rationalize later.

SMITH, WILLIAM KENNEDY:
The one Kennedy male found not guilty of taking advantage of a woman.

SOCIALIST:
Someone torn between the tragic failings of liberalism and the failing tragedy of Communism.

SOCIOPATH:
Someone so insane you don't want to risk calling him a nut.

"SOMETHING WICKED THIS WAY COMES":
What bouncers announce when they spot Ted Kennedy heading their way.

SOUNDBITE:
Snip of a speech or interview used in a TV news broadcast; usually a succinct, quotable remark.

Note: Should not be confused with sound*bile*, which most often refers to liberal commentator Molly Ivins.

SPECTER:

(1) A ghostly apparition. (2) A liberal who never had a ghost of a chance to win the Republican presidential nomination.

SPOTTED OWLS:

Birds perched in the wrong trees, and apparently they don't give a hoot.

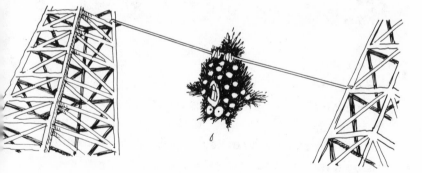

SPRINGER, JERRY:

TV talk show host who frequently focuses on salacious topics. A former mayor of Cincinnati, he went from being a man of the people to a man of the peephole.

STANFORD UNIVERSITY:
Where truth goes to die.

STATE DEPARTMENT:
Executive bureaucracy responsible for conducting foreign affairs. It's thought that Bill Clinton appointed a weak secretary of state because he hoped to conduct his own foreign affairs—whenever Hillary wasn't looking.

STATISTICS:
A collection of numbers you can't count on.

STATUS:

Social rank, best explained by Mark Twain: "In Boston, they ask, 'How much does he know?' In New York, 'How much is he worth?' In Philadelphia, 'Who were his parents?'" (And in Malibu, "Can he shoot the curl, dude?")

STEINEM, GLORIA:

Feminist writer who said, "A woman without a man is like a fish without a bicycle." This was thought to be a clever way of saying that women do not need men at all—a notion that must have been surprising to her father.

STEPHANOPOLOUS, GEORGE:

Political adviser to President Clinton. In Greek, his last name means "young snot with many bad hair days."

STONE, OLIVER:

Egotistical left-wing film director who fantasizes that the establishment conspired to kill President Kennedy. We would tell you more, but if we did, our lives might be in danger.

STONE, SHARON:

Actress who has starred in semiporn films and a $50,000-a-head fund-raiser for Bill Clinton. Anyone standing between them at the party was said to be between a rock and a hard place.

STRATEGIC DEFENSE INITIATIVE:

What liberals disparage as "Star Wars"—a plan to develop lasers, satellites, and other high technology devices to protect the United States against incoming nuclear missiles. Liberals passionately argued against research and development of the system for two reasons: (1) It might not work, and (2) It might work.

STRATEGY, DEMOCRATIC:

"We're not going to blow it this time. Just shut up, gays, women, and environmentalists. Just shut up. You'll get everything you want after the election.

But just, for the meantime, shut up so that we can win."

—*Congressman Peter Kostmayer (D-PA) at the Democratic National Convention in 1988*

STREISAND, BARBRA:

Liberal activist singer who proves that musical ability is located on the opposite side of the brain from rational thought. Ms. Streisand declared her feminism by burning the bra at the end of her first name: She is now called "Bar" by feminists, "Babs" by her fans, and "Blabs" by everyone else.

SUBCOMMITTEE:

Son of a committee. Called a "sub" committee because it's where deals are cut under the table.

SUPREME COURT:
Highest appellate court of the United States,
comprised of nine appointed judges serving for life,
any five of whom constitute a majority that can hand
down decisions designed to protect violent criminals
from the excesses of the innocent.

T

TAKING THE FIFTH:
(1) Claiming the constitutional right of the accused not
to incriminate one's self. (2) Ted Kennedy helping
himself at the local pub.

TALK RADIO:

Call-in programs with conservative hosts. Referred to by liberals as "hate radio" because the shows reflect the views and values of ordinary Americans, and liberals really hate that.

TASTELESS:

Liberal adjective for any joke that offends non-males, non-whites, or non-nuns.

TAX AND SPEND:

The crack cocaine of liberal politicians.

TECHNOLOGY:

Means used to develop objects for human comfort. "The marvels of modern technology include the development of a soda can which, when discarded, will last forever—and a $7,000 car, which, when properly cared for, will rust out in two or three years."

—*Paul Harwitz*

TEXAS:
"State with the largest fleet of armed pickup trucks in the world."

—*P. J. O'Rourke*

THERAPY:
Woody Allen's religion.

"THE TIMES THEY ARE A-CHANGIN'":
(1) Bob Dylan song (2) Democratic lament mourning the fact that the mayors of Los Angeles and New York are now both Republican. (Democrats could have sung instead, "The old gray mayors ain't what they used to be.")

THOMAS, CLARENCE:
Member of the U.S. Supreme Court whose nomination was hysterically opposed by liberals when research and eyewitness testimony revealed that he had knowingly committed conservatism.

THOMPSON, FRED:

Freshman Republican senator from Tennessee, former counsel to the Senate Watergate Committee, and a movie actor. (Now that Thompson and Sonny Bono have followed Ronald Reagan to Washington, only two conservatives are still being held in Hollywood.)

TIME MAGAZINE:

Liberal news-speak about the predictable, by the pretentious, for the perplexed.

TIME OFF FOR GOOD BEHAVIOR:

Shortening the sentence of a convicted criminal—a murderer, for example—by giving him credit for not murdering anyone else while imprisoned.

TOLERANCE:
Broad-mindedness about things like drug addiction, graffiti, and flag-burning, but not intolerable things like singing "Silent Night" in schools at Christmas.

TOUGH LOVE:
Double-dating with Dr. Joyce Brothers and Dr. Ruth Westheimer.

TRANSVESTITE:
Someone who goes from pumping up his sneakers to sneaking around in pumps.

TRASH TV:
The stuff between Hefty bag commercials.

TREKKIE:
Fanatical *Star Trek* fan trapped in a maturity warp.

TRIAL BY JURY:
What used to be deemed a guarantee of fair and impartial judgment. Now a guarantee of six figures if you get the right agent.

TRIAL LAWYERS:
A group of attorneys who are major contributors to Democratic politicians. In return, Democrats have created a legal and regulatory system so fiendishly complex that anyone dealing with it has to hire an attorney, thereby greatly increasing the income of lawyers. A case of "You scratch our back, and we'll back your scratch."

TRIVIAL PURSUIT:
The vice presidency.

TRUDEAU, GARY:
Liberal cartoonist who draws the comic strip "Doonesbury." Years ago, he took time off from his work—suspended animation—from which his sense of humor has yet to awaken.

TRULY NEEDY:
What liberals call welfare recipients who are so poor they can't even afford a second car.

TRUTH:
Spoken by a politician when not inconsistent with being elected.

TV:
An entertainment medium that idle eyes idolize.

TWEEDLEDUM, TWEEDLEDUMBER, TWEEDLEDUMBEST:
Phil Donahue, Connie Chung, and Elinor Clift.

U

UFO:

Unidentified Flying Object. Sometimes reported by Secret Service agents inside the White House, who usually spot them somewhere in the vicinity between Hillary's hand and Bill's head.

UNITED NATIONS:

A forum where the nations of the world gather to discuss serious problems—in particular, how to get the United States to increase its contributions so that everyone working for the United Nations can receive a pay raise.

UNITED STATES OF AMERICA:
A truly free nation, unless you're a taxpayer or want to buy something.

U.N. PEACEKEEPING:
"A convenient device for allowing the Great Powers to appear to be doing something where they do not really want to be doing anything."

—Charles Krauthammer

UP OR DOWN VOTE:
When the then Democrat-controlled Congress voted to keep the patronage jobs of congressional elevator operators who ran *automatic* elevators.

UTOPIA:
A liberal future when everyone drives a Volvo... wears Birkenstock sandals...lives in a rent-controlled apartment, with Mr. Rogers singing to the kids at the free day-care center...when the men have ponytails and the women don't...when the only ethnic humor is a nice Swedish joke once in a while...and when we're all on welfare, but no one is insensitive enough to call it that.

V

VEGETARIAN:
Someone who is inhumane to turnips.

VERMONT:
A large asylum for people not yet recovered from the '60s.

VICTIMOLOGY:
The core conviction that everyone is a victim, movingly expressed by Franklin D. Roosevelt: "I think we consider too much the good luck of the early bird,

and not enough of the bad luck of the early worm." To conservatives, the early bird is smart, talented, and industrious; to liberals, that's unfair.

VIRTUAL REALITY:
Computer's primitive approximation of the real world, sort of like Bill Clinton's views on foreign affairs.

V-J DAY:
Victory over Japan day, celebrating the end of World War II. The Clinton administration considered dropping the name for something politically correct, e.g., "Grant Reprieve, Overlook Villainy, Enjoy Life" day, or GROVEL for short.

WACO:
Where the Clinton Administration had many ironies in the fire.

WARHOL, ANDY:
Deceased American pop artist who said, "I am a deeply superficial person." Consequently, New York liberals worshipped him.

WALL STREET:
Las Vegas East.

WAR ON DRUGS:
Vietnam.

WASHINGTON, DC:
(1) City called the "seat" of the federal government because so many asses sit in it. (2) "The only city where sound travels faster than light."

—*Ronald Reagan*

WAXMAN, HENRY:
Liberal congressman (D-CA) and a common House pest who would like to regulate everything but the cutting of nostril hair.

WHAM:
White Hetero Angry Males. The one group without its own caucus in the Democratic Party, because there aren't enough of them remaining to constitute a quorum.

"WHAT'S THE FREQUENCY, KENNETH?":
Question shouted repeatedly at Dan Rather as he was assaulted by a crazed man on a street in New York. The attacker was set free by the court on the grounds that no one who attacked Dan Rather could possibly be crazy.

WHINING:
Liberal self-expression.

WHITEWATER:
Bill Clinton in a raft of trouble.

WHOLESOME:
Word that liberals use mockingly in talking about people, but reverently when talking about health food.

WILLIS, BRUCE:
A die-hard Republican.

WOMAN'S MOVIE:
"One where the woman commits adultery all through the picture, and, at the end, her husband begs her to forgive him."

—*Oscar Levant*

XENOPHOBIA:
Fear or loathing of foreigners, exemplified in this passage from *To England with Love,* by David Frost and Antony Jay: "There have been many definitions of hell, but for the English the best definition is that it is a place where the Germans are the police, the Swedish are the comedians, the Italians are the defence force, Frenchmen dig the roads, the Belgians are the pop singers, the Spanish run the railways, the Turks cook the food, the Irish are the waiters, the Greeks run the government and the common language is Dutch."

YUGO:

An automobile deported from Yugoslavia.

"YOU PEOPLE":

Phrase used by Ross Perot when addressing the National Association for the Advancement of Colored People. It caused an uproar among delegates who wanted him to say, "Us blacks."

ZIPPER, WIN ONE FOR THE:

The campaign slogan for Bill Clinton's reelection.

—*Rush Limbaugh*